The Game of Chess

By Carlo Goldoni

A translation from the French of
Le Bourru bienfaisant (1771)
by Simon Thomas

Copyright © 2013 Simon Thomas
All rights reserved

For performance rights contact the author on
simont@bubblechamber.net

ISBN-10: 1489556060
ISBN-13: 978-1489556066

The Game of Chess

Introduction

The Game of Chess is a translation of Carlo Goldoni's penultimate play, *Le Bourru bienfaisant,* written in French in 1771, when he was living in exile in Paris. Goldoni (1707-1793) idolized Molière and desperately wanted to have a success at the Comédie-Française, the so-called *maison de Molière.* With *Le Bourru bienfaisant,* he fulfilled his wish, although he was not so lucky with his final comedy, *L'avare fastueux,* a poorer piece, which got a less positive reception.

What he did with both of these final plays was build the plot around an oxymoronic central character. The original title of the play translates as "The Beneficent Boor." The boor of the title is Monsieur Géronte, an ill-tempered old gentleman with a heart of gold. The protagonist of the final play is a miser who always puts on a show of extravagance and then whips the silver away when no-one's looking (the title *L'avare fastueux* means *The Ostentatious Miser*).

The Game of Chess is a play full of nice people, flawed and foolish perhaps but all good at heart. Géronte rants and raves, and goes so

The Game of Chess

far as to push his servant Picard over in temper, but is horrified by his own actions, picks him up, apologises and gives him money for the doctor. He's unpredictable and irascible but always has his friends and family's best interests at heart.

His nephew and wife, Monsieur and Madame Dalancour, and his niece, the unmarried Angélique, all live with him in a chateau close to Paris. As well as the devoted manservant Picard, there's a gossipy housekeeper Marton and another loveable character, Géronte's friend Dorval, with whom he likes to play chess. He's the person most able to deal with the old man. Angélique is courted by a young gentleman called Valère.

The play is short and light-hearted, full of good humour and human feeling. The characters are well drawn, believable and charming. The crux of the play is Géronte's personality. The others have to catch him at the right time because he's always ready to fly of the handle. When he's in full possession of the facts, though, Géronte is quick to do the right thing.

The Game of Chess

The game of chess is an essential indicator of his nature. It's when he's alone, thinking through the game (and manipulating the chess pieces to do what he wants) that he's most content. When he tries to move people around as he does the pawns and rooks, he finds them less easy to control. His behaviour is not malicious; he just finds objects more pleasing and easier to deal with than the capriciousness and unpredictability of flesh and blood people.

There's a freshness and good feeling in *Le Bourru bienfaisant* that is missing in the following play. It was enough to make it a success on the stage, while *L'avare fastueux* was destined to flop. Sadly, these were to be his final works for the stage and Goldoni died in poverty in 1793.

A note on the translation:

The Game of Chess is a free translation of Le Bourru bienfaisant, made directly from the original. with language that is intended to be speakable but not too colloquial. The French names have been retained and there are no changes in the plot or characterisations.

For my friend Mark Valencia, a continuing source of encouragement

The Game of Chess

Characters

Monsieur Geronte

Angelique, *his niece*

Monsieur Dalancour, *his nephew*

Madame Dalancour

Valere, *in love with Angelique*

Dorval, *friend to Monsieur Geronte*

Marton, *Monsieur Geronte's housekeeper*

Picard, *Monsieur Geronte's manservant*

Servant to the household

The plays is set in a chateau in Paris, 1771

The Game of Chess

Act One

ANGELIQUE: Go Valere, please. We mustn't be caught!

VALERE: Oh, my darling!

MARTON: Listen to her. Off you go now.

VALERE: But, I just want to make sure…

MARTON: *(Sighing)* Make sure of what? Come on, off with you.

VALERE: That she still loves me. And only me.

ANGELIQUE: How can you doubt it. Of course I do.

VALERE: That's all I needed to know.

MARTON: Oh, she loves you alright. Now get out of here before my master comes.

The Game of Chess

ANGELIQUE: But my uncle's never about at this time.

MARTON: True, but this is his favourite room. It's where he likes to relax. He's always here, pacing about or playing chess. *(To Valere)*. You don't know what he's like monsieur.

ANGELIQUE: Well, it's true I've never met him but my father knew him well. He told me all about him.

MARTON: Unless you know Monsieur Geronte you can't understand. He's a good man. He can be very kind and generous but sometimes….. let's say, he can be a bit difficult.

ANGELIQUE: Yes, he tells me he loves me, and I'm sure he does, but he terrifies me.

VALERE: But what have you got to fear? Your brother is your guardian, not your uncle. And Dalancour is a good friend of mine. I'll have a word with him.

MARTON: Oh yes, you can rely on Monsieur Dalancour!

The Game of Chess

VALERE: What are you saying? That he'd turn me down?

MARTON: I should say so.

VALERE: What do you mean?

MARTON: Look. *(To Angelique)* My nephew is the new clerk at your brother's lawyers and he said… now, don't breathe a word of this… he said it in the strictest confidence… you mustn't breathe a word of this…

ANGELIQUE: *(impatiently)* Oh, get on with it.

VALERE: You've got nothing to fear from us.

MARTON: *(In a whisper)* Well, they say Monsieur Dalancour is a… ruined man. He's squandered his whole fortune, and your dowry, and he's up to his eyes in debt. *(To Angelique)* You've become a real problem for him and what I've heard is…. that he intends sending you to the convent.

ANGELIQUE: What? That can't be true!

The Game of Chess

VALERE: It's not possible! I've known Dalancour for a long time. He's always been so sensible and honest. He gets a bit carried away sometimes…

MARTON: A bit carried away! You can say that again. He takes after his uncle in that. But he doesn't have Monsieur Geronte's kindness. Far from it…

VALERE: But everyone respects and admires him. His father had every reason to be proud of him.

MARTON: Oh, monsieur, he's never been the same since he married that woman.

VALERE: What, you mean it's Madame Dalancour who…

MARTON: Oh yes, she's the problem to be sure. Monsieur Geronte only falls out with his nephew over her. I can't be sure, but I think it's her who's had this idea of the convent.

ANGELIQUE: What are you saying? My sister-in-

The Game of Chess

	law? I've always found her so reasonable and she treats me with the greatest kindness.
VALERE:	She's always so gentle. I can't believe it.
MARTON:	Just look at how she dresses, monsieur, and the jewellery! She has to be first with every fashion and she's always gallivanting off to balls and plays. I'll say no more.
VALERE:	But her husband's always at her side.
ANGELIQUE:	Yes, my brother never leaves her.
MARTON:	With respect, mademoiselle, they are both fools and they're both going to ruin themselves.
VALERE:	I don't believe it's possible.
MARTON:	Well, you asked and now you know. You should go. You mustn't expose mademoiselle to danger. Her uncle's

The Game of Chess

 | |
---|---
 | the only one who can get her out of this mess and she mustn't go upsetting him.
VALERE: | Try not to worry, my darling. We'll sort this out one way or another.
MARTON: | Ssh, I can hear someone coming. Go, monsieur. *(Valere leaves)*
ANGELIQUE: | I'm so unhappy!
MARTON: | It's your uncle coming. Told you so.
ANGELIQUE: | I must go.
MARTON: | On the contrary, you must stay and face him. Just open your heart to him.
ANGELIQUE: | But he's so scary. I'd rather put my hand in the fire!
MARTON: | Come, my dear, be brave. He may be ill-tempered sometimes but he's not unkind.
ANGELIQUE: | You're his housekeeper and he trusts

The Game of Chess

	you. Please speak to him on my behalf.
MARTON:	Absolutely not. You must speak to him yourself. What I will do is prepare him for you. Let me have a word first.
ANGELIQUE:	Yes, please say something to him. Then it won't be so hard for me. *(Going)*
MARTON:	Don't go far.
ANGELIQUE:	No, I promise. I'll be nearby. *(She leaves)*
MARTON:	*(Alone)* She's a good girl and I do love her. I saw her born and I want to see her happy. Ah, here's Monsieur Geronte. Here goes.
GERONTE:	*(Entering)* Picard!
MARTON:	Monsieur…
GERONTE:	Tell Picard I want him.

The Game of Chess

MARTON: Of course, monsieur. But first could I have a word?

GERONTE: *(Brusquely)* Picard, Picard!

MARTON: *(Bad-temperedly)* Picard, Picard!

PICARD: *(Entering)* I'm coming, I'm coming.

MARTON: The master…

PICARD: Monsieur?

GERONTE: Go to my friend Dorval and tell him I'm waiting for him to finish our game of chess.

PICARD: Yes, monsieur, but…

GERONTE: What is it?

PICARD: I have something to ask you.

GERONTE: Well, what is it?

PICARD: Your nephew, monsieur…

The Game of Chess

GERONTE: *(Sharply)* Fetch Monsieur Dorval!

PICARD: He'd like to speak to you…

GERONTE: Off with you, you rascal!

PICARD: What a master! *(Leaves)*

GERONTE: *(Approaching the table)* The fool! The wretch! No, I won't speak to him. I don't want him coming here disturbing my peace.

MARTON: *(Aside)* Now, he's in a proper old mood. I won't get anywhere with him.

GERONTE: *(Sitting)* Bad game yesterday. Very bad! How could I have been checkmated when it was going so well? Tut! Let's see now. *(Looking at the chessboard)* I haven't slept a wink all night thinking about it.

MARTON: Monsieur, might I have a word?

GERONTE: No!

MARTON: No? It's something that's sure to

The Game of Chess

interest you.

GERONTE: Well, then, what is it? Spit it out.

MARTON: Your niece would like a word with you.

GERONTE: Everyone would it seems! I'm sorry, I don't have the time.

MARTON: Very well. *(Pause)* You're doing something important, are you?

GERONTE: Yes, very important. I don't get much pleasure. I try to amuse myself and everyone plagues me with problems.

MARTON: The poor girl…

GERONTE: What's the matter with her?

MARTON: They want to put her in a convent.

GERONTE: *(Rising)* Who does? What do you mean? Who's going to put my niece in a convent? Without my consent? Without my say so?

The Game of Chess

MARTON: You know of Monsieur Dalancour's affairs?

GERONTE: I have nothing to do with my nephew's affairs, or those of his damned wife. It's his fortune. If he wants to squander it, that's his look out. But, as for my niece, I'm the head of this family and I'll decide what's to become of her.

MARTON: Oh, monsieur, I'm so pleased to see you take an interest in her. I truly fear for her, you know.

GERONTE: Where is she now?

MARTON: She's in the next room, monsieur, waiting for her chance to put her case to you.

GERONTE: Send her in.

MARTON: Thank you, monsieur. She'll appreciate your concern. But…

GERONTE: But what?

The Game of Chess

MARTON: She's shy, monsieur…

GERONTE: So?

MARTON: If you speak to her…

GERONTE: *(Irritably)* I thought you wanted me to speak to her!

MARTON: Yes, but this tone of voice…

GERONTE: My tone of voice never hurt anyone. Tell her to come and listen to what I have to say, not the tone of my voice.

MARTON: You're right, monsieur. I know you. You are so good and kind and charitable, but… please treat her gently. She's only a child. Speak to her with a little tenderness.

GERONTE: Yes, you're right. I'll be gentle with her.

MARTON: You promise me, now?

GERONTE: I promise.

The Game of Chess

MARTON: Don't forget.

GERONTE: I won't forget!

MARTON: And, most of all, don't lose your patience.

GERONTE: *(Sharply)* All right, I've said so, haven't I?

MARTON: *(Leaving)* Poor Angelique. I do worry for her.

GERONTE: *(Alone)* She's right, I get carried away sometimes. My dear little niece deserves a little gentleness, bless her. *(Angelique approaches timidly)* Come, my dear.

ANGELIQUE: *(Holding back)* Monsieur…

GERONTE: *(Getting impatient)* How can I talk to you, if we're a league apart?

ANGELIQUE: *(Trembling)* Excuse me, monsieur…

GERONTE: *(Gently)* What do you want to say?

The Game of Chess

ANGELIQUE: *(Hesitantly)* Has Marton said anything to you?

GERONTE: *(Beginning gently but getting worked up as he goes on)* Yes, she has said something. She's said that your brother, the fool, that indulgent idiot has let that wife of his lead him by the nose, until he's ruined himself and that she's brought him to nothing... My God! He has no respect for me! *(Angelique backs away)* Where are you going?

ANGELIQUE: *(Trembling)* I see you're angry, monsieur...

GERONTE: What if I am? If I'm angry with that dunce of a brother of yours, what's that to you? I'm not angry with you. *(Calming a little)* Come, talk to me. You mustn't be afraid of my temper.

ANGELIQUE: Dearest uncle, I... don't know how to speak to you... when you're like this.

GERONTE: *(Controlling himself)* Here, I'm perfectly calm. Come, speak, my dear.

The Game of Chess

ANGELIQUE: Monsieur.... Marton will have told you...

GERONTE: Never mind what Marton has told me. I want to hear it from you.

ANGELIQUE: *(Timidly)* My brother...

GERONTE: Yes, yes. Your brother...

ANGELIQUE: ... wants to send me to a convent.

GERONTE: Well, do you want to go to a convent?

ANGELIQUE: But, monsieur...

GERONTE: *(Quickly)* Well?

ANGELIQUE: It's not for me to decide.

GERONTE: *(Sharply)* I didn't say that it was, but I want to know how you feel about it.

ANGELIQUE: Please, monsieur, you're frightening me.

GERONTE: *(Aside)* It's outrageous! *(Controlling himself)* Come my dear, I understand.

The Game of Chess

                You don't like the idea of the convent?

ANGELIQUE: No, monsieur.

GERONTE: What would you prefer to do?

ANGELIQUE: *(Hesitantly)* Monsieur…

GERONTE: Have no fear, I'm quite calm. You can speak freely.

ANGELIQUE: *(Aside)* I can't go through with this.

GERONTE: Come here. Would you like to be married?

ANGELIQUE: Monsieur…

GERONTE: Yes or no?

ANGELIQUE: If that's what you want…

GERONTE: *(Impatiently)* Yes or no?

ANGELIQUE: Well…. Yes.

The Game of Chess

GERONTE: *(Getting worked up)* Yes? Yes? You want to get married, throw away your freedom, lose your peace of mind? Oh, well, so much the worse for you. Fine! If that's what you want I'll marry you off.

ANGELIQUE: *(Aside)* Beneath all his anger, he means well.

GERONTE: *(Brusquely)* Is there anyone you have in mind?

ANGELIQUE: *(Aside)* Dare I tell him of Valere?

GERONTE: Well? Do you have some lover tucked away?

ANGELIQUE: *(Aside)* Now's not the moment. Marton must break the news to him.

GERONTE: *(Really worked up)* Come, come, give me an answer. I wouldn't have thought, living as you do, with those people, that you'd have had the chance to meet anyone. Tell me the truth. I'll do the right thing, as long as you

The Game of Chess

	deserve it. Do you hear?
ANGELIQUE:	*(Trembling)* Yes, monsieur.
GERONTE:	Speak up, then. Is there someone?
ANGELIQUE:	*(Confused)* But... no, monsieur... there's no-one.
GERONTE:	So be it. I will find you a husband.
ANGELIQUE:	*(Aside)* Oh, what have I done? *(Aloud)* Please monsieur...
GERONTE:	What is it?
ANGELIQUE:	You know how timid I am...
GERONTE:	Yes, yes. I know you women. Here you are, a dove but once you're married, you'll become a dragon!
ANGELIQUE:	Oh, uncle. You are so good, so kind...
GERONTE:	Enough now. *(He turns away)*

The Game of Chess

ANGELIQUE: May I say something else?

GERONTE: *(At the chessboard)* Where's Dorval got to?

ANGELIQUE: Please, uncle, may I…

GERONTE: *(Occupied with the game)* You may leave.

ANGELIQUE: Just one word more…

GERONTE: *(annoyed)* It's all been said.

ANGELIQUE: *(Aside)* Oh, heavens! I'm even more unhappy than I was before. What will become of me? Ah, I must find Marton. She won't abandon me. *(Leaves)*

GERONTE: *(Alone)* She's a good girl. I'd like to see her happy. Even if there were some lover, I'd do my best to please her. But there isn't. So, let me see. Who could I find for her? Where the devil's Dorval? Why isn't he here? I can't wait to see how this game turns out. That damned move lost me the game yesterday. I should have won,

The Game of Chess

I'm sure of it. I must have lost my concentration. Now, let's see... this was the arrangement... this piece here... and so... there, that was Dorval's game. My king takes his rook. His bishop next to his king... and I... check! Yes, and I take the pawn... Now Dorval's turn... did he take my bishop? Yes, he did. My bishop and I... double check with my knight. Good God! Dorval's lost his queen! He plays his king, I take his queen. The fool! With his king he takes my knight. So much the worse for him. Got him in a trap! Checked by my king... my queen, yes there... checkmate! Got it. Yes, it's easy. Checkmate... I've won the game. Ha! If Dorval were here, I'd soon show him. *(Calling)* Picard! *(Dalancour approaches)*

DALANCOUR: *(Aside, awkward)* My uncle's alone. If I could just get him to listen to me.

GERONTE: So, let's arrange the game as it was. *(Calling louder)* Picard!

The Game of Chess

DALANCOUR: Monsieur…

GERONTE: *(Not turning and thinking he's talking to Picard)* Well? Did you find Dorval?

DORVAL: *(Entering)* Here I am, my friend.

DALANCOUR: Uncle…

(Monsieur Geronte turns, sees Dalancour, rises brusquely, turning his chair over. He leaves abruptly without saying a word)

DORVAL: *(Smiling)* What was all that about?

DALANCOUR: How dreadful! That little show was for my benefit.

DORVAL: My friend Geronte is his usual self, I see.

DALANCOUR: I can only apologise for my uncle.

DORVAL: I seem to have arrived at a bad time.

DALANCOUR: *(Embarrassed)* You must excuse my uncle's behaviour.

The Game of Chess

DORVAL: *(Smiling)* I'll give him a good telling off when he comes back.

DALANCOUR: Oh, my good friend, if you could put in a word for me…

DORVAL: I'd like to help, if I could, but…

DALANCOUR: *(Worked up)* He has nothing but reproaches for me. If he knew the truth, he'd understand me better.

DORVAL: Yes, I sympathise with your situation. Anyone would. But Madame Dalancour…

DALANCOUR: My wife, monsieur? Oh, you do not know her. Everyone is wrong about her, and my uncle in particular. I must tell you the truth; it's only fair that I do. She knows nothing of my troubles. Really, she has no idea. She has always believed me to be richer than I am and I've never revealed the true situation to her. You see, I love her and I've never denied her anything. We married young and I've

The Game of Chess

always given her what she wants. And what she deserves. That's what has brought about my ruin.

DORVAL: Ah, to please a woman. That's no small task.

DALANCOUR: I'm sure that, if she'd known the situation, she'd be the first to cut her spending.

DORVAL: She's never tried to curb your extravagances, my friend.

DALANCOUR: *(Emphatically)* That's because she doesn't know my situation!

DORVAL: *(Chuckling)* My poor friend!

DALANCOUR: *(Irritated)* What is it?

DORVAL: I'm just sorry for you, that's all.

DALANCOUR: Are you laughing at me?

DORVAL: No, no. But... look, you do love your wife, don't you?

The Game of Chess

DALANCOUR: *(Really worked up)* I've told you I do. I have always loved her and I always will. I know her. Other people don't and I won't have them saying bad things about her.

DORVAL: *(Seriously)* Gently my friend, gently. You must learn to control this family temper.

DALANCOUR: Please forgive me. I'd hate to upset you, of all people. But, when it comes to my wife...

DORVAL: Now, now. Let's say no more about it.

DALANCOUR: But I want you to believe me.

DORVAL: *(Coolly)* I do, my friend.

DALANCOUR: But you don't. I can see. You're not convinced.

DORVAL: *(Sharply)* Excuse me. I'm telling the truth. I do believe you.

The Game of Chess

DALANCOUR: I'm sorry, please forgive me. And, dear friend, if you could speak to my uncle on my behalf…

DORVAL: I'll do my best.

DALANCOUR: I'm indebted to you.

DORVAL: You will need to tell me more. How did you get yourself in this situation? And so soon. It's only four years since your father died. I believe he left you a considerable fortune. You can't have spent it all, already.

DALANCOUR: *(Miserably)* Oh, if you only knew the bad luck I've had. Things were going badly and I tried to put them right but, in the process, I made them worse. I did a bit of this and a bit of that. I've speculated and invested, and now it seems I've lost the lot.

DORVAL: Ah, I see. Bad advice, eh? You're not the first to be ruined that way.

DALANCOUR: And now it's all over.

The Game of Chess

DORVAL: I'm afraid it looks like it, my friend. It's particularly sad for your sister.

DALANCOUR: *(Guiltily)* I can't think of giving her a dowry now but I've come up with a solution. She's to go to the convent.

DORVAL: You could do that but have you spoken to your uncle about it?

DALANCOUR: He won't listen to me. If you could speak to him for me, you'll be speaking for Angelique too. Promise me that you'll talk to him. For her sake.

DORVAL: I'll do my best. Do you know where he is now?

DALANCOUR: I'll find out. *(Calling)* Hello! Is anyone there? *(To Dorval)* You know how he respects you. He loves you and listens to you. He surely won't refuse you.

DORVAL: I'm not so sure about that.

The Game of Chess

DALANCOUR: Well, I am. Please do your best with him.

PICARD: *(Entering)* Here, monsieur.

DALANCOUR: Has my uncle gone out?

PICARD: No, monsieur, he's in the garden.

DALANCOUR: In the garden? At this time of day?

PICARD: He likes to walk there when he's in a temper. The air does him good.

DORVAL: I think I'll join him.

DALANCOUR: No, I think it would be best to let my uncle calm down a bit. It would be better to wait.

DORVAL: He may go out and not come back.

PICARD: There's not much danger of that. A quarter of an hour will do. *(To Dorval)* Besides, when he finds you here, he'll be himself again.

DALANCOUR: Well, my friend, you wait in his room. He'll join you there by and by.

The Game of Chess

DORVAL: Very well. I can see your problem and it needs sorting out. I'll do what I can. *(He goes into M. Geronte's room)*

DALANCOUR: You didn't get a chance to speak to my uncle then?

PICARD: I'm sorry, monsieur, I tried but he wouldn't listen.

DALANCOUR: This is hopeless. Please let me know when you think it's a good time to approach him. I'll show my thanks… when I can, I promise.

PICARD: Thank you, monsieur, but there's nothing I need.

DALANCOUR: Are you rich then?

PICARD: No, not rich. But I have a good and kind master. I have a wife and four children and Monsieur Geronte makes sure I'm looked after. We eat well and want for nothing. *(Leaves)*

DALANCOUR: *(Alone)* Oh, my uncle is a good man.

The Game of Chess

I'm sure he'll help me if he can… if he knew the full facts. But my wife mustn't know… Oh, why have I deceived her? And why do I deceive myself? My uncle won't come round. I must go. Every second counts. My lawyer is waiting for me. Problems, problems, problems. He says he can buy me time… but it's more than I can bear. Too much suffering. And, what's more, my honour is at stake. This won't end well. *(as he is leaving, Madame Dalancour approaches)* My wife!

MADAME DALANCOUR:	Ah, there you are, my dear. I've been looking for you everywhere.
DALANCOUR:	I'm just going out…
MADAME DALANCOUR:	I've just run into the old bear… and how he was growling!
DALANCOUR:	You mean my uncle?
MADAME DALANCOUR:	Yes. The sun was shining, so I thought I'd take a stroll in the garden. There he was, pacing up and down

The Game of Chess

and talking to himself at the top of his voice. Tell me, is his servant married?

DALANCOUR: *(Puzzled)* Yes.

MADAME DALANCOUR: That must be it then. He was talking about a man and his wife, and he didn't have a good word to say about them.

DALANCOUR: *(Aside)* No servant, I think!

MADAME DALANCOUR: He really is an unbearable old man.

DALANCOUR: He's my uncle and you should show him some respect.

MADAME DALANCOUR: Has he any reason for not liking me? I do show him respect but it's not returned. I mock him sometimes but that's just between you and me. You don't really mind, do you? The rest of the time, I'm polite towards him but I get nothing but rudeness back. What could be the cause of that?

38

The Game of Chess

	He's so rude to us, and to me especially. Why does he find it so difficult to be courteous?
DALANCOUR:	*(Embarrassed)* But... we must be always respectful to him... he is my uncle, after all... we may find we need him one day.
MADAME DALANCOUR:	Us? Need him? I can't see why. We're perfectly well off. We live within our means, don't we? If we carry on that way, I can't see why we'd need his, or anyone's help.
DALANCOUR:	Perfectly well off!
MADAME DALANCOUR:	Why, yes. I've never asked you for anything we don't have, have I?
DALANCOUR:	*(Aside)* How miserable I am!
MADAME DALANCOUR:	What's the matter? You seem troubled. You're not your usual self.
DALANCOUR:	No, you're mistaken. I'm fine.

The Game of Chess

MADAME
DALANCOUR: Excuse me, but I know you, my dear. If there's something wrong, I should know about it.

DALANCOUR: *(Very embarrassed)* It's… my sister… that's all.

MADAME
DALANCOUR: Your sister? What on earth's the problem with her? She's the best child in the world. Look, leave it to me and I'll deal with her. I know what will make her happy.

DALANCOUR: And what's that?

MADAME
DALANCOUR: You've decided she should go to the convent. I haven't said anything until now but I think you should drop the idea. It can't be what she wants.

DALANCOUR: *(Annoyed)* She doesn't know what she wants at her age.

MADAME
DALANCOUR: But you can't just impose your will on her. You should think of getting her married instead.

The Game of Chess

DALANCOUR: She's too young.

MADAME DALANCOUR: She's the age I was when we married.

DALANCOUR: What do you want me to do? Go from door to door begging for a husband?

MADAME DALANCOUR: Don't get upset, my dear, please. Unless I'm mistaken, your friend Valere has his eye on her. And I think she feels the same.

DALANCOUR: *(Aside)* Oh, this is not what I want to hear.

MADAME DALANCOUR: He's a good man. Could there be a better match for Angelique?

DALANCOUR: I don't know. I can't discuss it now.

MADAME DALANCOUR: Please, my dear. You've never denied me anything. Just do this for me. Give Angelique to him. It would make me so happy.

The Game of Chess

DALANCOUR: *(Very awkward)* Madame…

MADAME DALANCOUR: Well?

DALANCOUR: It's just not possible.

MADAME DALANCOUR: Why ever not?

DALANCOUR: It's my uncle… he'd never give his consent.

MADAME DALANCOUR: Now, listen. I'm quite happy to show your uncle the respect that's due to him, but you are Angelique's brother. Her dowry is in your hands, so it's up to you. If I'm right about her feelings, you should leave everything to me.

DALANCOUR: No! Just drop the matter, will you?

MADAME DALANCOUR: Don't you want your sister to be happy?

DALANCOUR: On the contrary.

The Game of Chess

MADAME DALANCOUR: *(To herself)* Could it be that...

DALANCOUR: I have to go out. We'll speak about it later.

MADAME DALANCOUR: Do you not want me involved? Is that it?

DALANCOUR: Not at all.

MADAME DALANCOUR: Is it to do with the dowry?

DALANCOUR: I can't talk about it now. *(Leaves)*

MADAME DALANCOUR: *(Alone)* What does this mean? I don't understand. Could my husband be... No, he's above reproach. But his behaviour is very odd.

ANGELIQUE: *(Entering)* I must find Marton.

MADAME DALANCOUR: Sister.

ANGELIQUE: *(Vexed)* Madame.

The Game of Chess

MADAME DALANCOUR: Angelique, where are you going?

ANGELIQUE: Out, madame.

MADAME DALANCOUR: Are you upset?

ANGELIQUE: Perhaps.

MADAME DALANCOUR: With me?

ANGELIQUE: Madame...

MADAME DALANCOUR: Listen, Angelique. If it's this idea of sending you to the convent, you must believe that I had nothing to do with it. On the contrary, I want you to be happy and I'll do anything I can to help you.

ANGELIQUE: *(Aside, crying)* How false she is. How she tries to deceive me.

MADAME DALANCOUR: What is it, dear? Why are you crying?

The Game of Chess

ANGELIQUE: It's… my brother. Him and his problems.

MADAME DALANCOUR: *(Astonished)* What do you mean, his problems?

ANGELIQUE: Nobody knows more about them than you.

MADAME DALANCOUR: I don't understand. What are you talking about?

ANGELIQUE: It's not worth it.

GERONTE: *(Entering from the garden)* Picard!

PICARD: *(Coming from M Geronte's room)* Here, monsieur.

GERONTE: Where's Dorval?

PICARD: He's in your room, monsieur.

GERONTE: In my room? And you didn't tell me?

PICARD: Monsieur, I haven't had the chance.

The Game of Chess

GERONTE: *(Sees Angelique and Mme Dalancour. Speaks to Angelique but from time to time turns and directs his words at Mme Dalancour)* What are you doing here? This is my salon. I don't want women here. Not you or any of your family. Go away.

ANGELIQUE: *(Upset)* Oh, uncle...

GERONTE: Go away, I said. *(Angelique leaves in tears)*

MADAME DALANCOUR: Excuse me, monsieur...

GERONTE: What a nuisance! Impertinent child. She's always bothering me. I'm going to have to have this door locked. I can use the other staircase.

MADAME DALANCOUR: Please don't get annoyed, uncle. You needn't put yourself out on my behalf.

GERONTE: *(Wanting to enter his room but not wanting*

The Game of Chess

to pass Madame Dalancour. To Picard)
Dorval is in my room, you say?

PICARD: Yes, monsieur.

MADAME DALANCOUR: *(Stepping back)* Please, uncle, don't let me get in your way.

GERONTE: *(Nodding in her direction)* Your servant. Yes, I'll have that door blocked up. *(He enters his room, followed by Picard)*

MADAME DALANCOUR: *(Alone)* What a misery guts! But it's not him who's bothering me now. It's my husband. What are these problems Angelique is talking about? I'm very worried. I fear… I want to know the truth but I'm afraid of what I may discover.

End of Act One

The Game of Chess

Act Two

GERONTE: Come on, let's play and do stop your chattering.

DORVAL: But it concerns your nephew.

GERONTE: He's a fool, an imbecile, a slave to that wife of his and a victim of his own vanity.

DORVAL: Calm down, old friend, calm down.

GERONTE: And you're as bad with your "calm down."

DORVAL: I'm only trying to help.

GERONTE: *(Sitting)* Sit, and let's get on with the game.

DORVAL: Poor fellow!

The Game of Chess

GERONTE: Now, where were we?

DORVAL: *(Muttering)* You'll be the one that loses in the end.

GERONTE: Nonsense. I've got it all worked out. Just see.

DORVAL: You'll lose him, I tell you.

GERONTE: Oh, I don't think so.

DORVAL: If you don't help him out, he'll never forgive you.

GERONTE: Who?

DORVAL: Your nephew.

GERONTE: What? I'm talking about the game. Sit down and let's begin.

DORVAL: *(Sitting)* Yes, I want to play but listen to me first.

GERONTE: Are you still going on about that fool Dalancour?

The Game of Chess

DORVAL: You've got to help him, you know.

GERONTE: I'm not listening.

DORVAL: Do you hate him?

GERONTE: No, I don't hate anyone.

DORVAL: But if you won't…

GERONTE: Enough of this! Play the game or I'll leave the room.

DORVAL: Let me say one thing and then I'll stop.

GERONTE: Give me patience!

DORVAL: You're not badly off.

GERONTE: Yes. I thank God.

DORVAL: You have more than you need.

GERONTE: Yes.

The Game of Chess

DORVAL: And yet you won't give anything to your nephew?

GERONTE: Not a penny.

DORVAL: Therefore…

GERONTE: Therefore what?

DORVAL: Therefore, you must hate him.

GERONTE: Therefore you don't know what you're talking about. What I hate is the way he carries on. Ludicrous behaviour. If I gave him money, it would just encourage his vanity and excess. Let him mend his ways and then I'll help him. If he repents, I'll think about it. But if I bail him out now, he'll go back and do it all over again.

DORVAL: *(Thinks for a moment and appears convinced)* Right, let's play.

GERONTE: About time too.

The Game of Chess

DORVAL: *(After playing for a moment).* No, this won't do.

GERONTE: Check!

DORVAL: Poor girl!

(A long silence while they both think about the game)

GERONTE: Who?

DORVAL: Angelique.

GERONTE: Now, that's something else. You can talk to me about her. *(Stops playing)*

DORVAL: She's very unhappy, you know.

GERONTE: I've thought about that and I've decided she should be married.

DORVAL: Excellent, my friend. That's a good solution.

GERONTE: She's a fine girl, eh? Beautiful and well-behaved.

The Game of Chess

DORVAL: She is.

GERONTE: The man who marries her is a lucky one. *(he thinks for a moment and then rises quickly)* Dorval!

DORVAL: Geronte?

GERONTE: Listen.

DORVAL: Well?

GERONTE: You're a good friend.

DORVAL: I'd like to think so.

GERONTE: Why don't I give Angelique to you?

DORVAL: What?

GERONTE: Yes, my dear little niece. You shall have her!

DORVAL: Now, wait a minute… what?

GERONTE: What do you mean? Am I not talking clearly? I'm saying that, if you want her, she's yours.

The Game of Chess

DORVAL: *(Shocked)* I...

GERONTE: And what's more, in addition to the dowry, I'll give you 100,000 francs of my own. Eh? What do you say to that?

DORVAL: Dear Geronte, this is too much. Too much, too quickly.

GERONTE: I know you. You'll be perfect for her. What do you say?

DORVAL: But...

GERONTE: What now?

DORVAL: What about her brother?

GERONTE: Her brother! He's nothing. It's my decision not his. I'm the head of this family. Now, what do you say?

DORVAL: Slow down, old friend. This isn't the sort of thing you can rush. I have to think about it.

The Game of Chess

GERONTE: What's the problem? If you can love her and if she suits you, it's a deal.

DORVAL: *(Shocked)* But…

GERONTE: Stop it with the buts.

DORVAL: Have you thought of the fact that she's 16 and I'm nearly 45?

GERONTE: So what? You're still a young man and Angelique's a sensible girl.

DORVAL: Well, there may be someone else she prefers.

GERONTE: There isn't.

DORVAL: How do you know?

GERONTE: I know. Come along now, I'll go straight to my lawyer. He'll have a contract drawn up in no time. The girl's yours.

DORVAL: Please, my friend, not so fast.

The Game of Chess

GERONTE: For goodness' sake. What's the matter? Are you trying to annoy me? This reticence is tiring. Make your mind up.

DORVAL: Is this really what you want?

GERONTE: Yes, it is. I'm giving you a lovely girl, who's wise, honest and good. You're getting 100,000 francs for a dowry and the same again as a wedding present. What on earth can be the problem with that?

DORVAL: I don't deserve all this.

GERONTE: Nonsense. This modesty is getting on my nerves.

DORVAL: Don't get upset, now. I have to be sure about this.

GERONTE: There's nothing more to discuss.

DORVAL: In that case, the answer's yes.

GERONTE: At last!

The Game of Chess

DORVAL: There's just one condition.

GERONTE: What's that?

DORVAL: Angelique has to want it too.

GERONTE: Is that all?

DORVAL: That's all.

GERONTE: In that case, there's no problem. You can be sure of that.

DORVAL: Then I'm very happy.

GERONTE: I am too. Come here; embrace me. Nephew!

DORVAL: *(Laughing)* Uncle!

(Dalancour enters but, seeing his uncle, he holds back and listens)

GERONTE: *(Calling)* Picard! *(To Dorval)* This is the happiest day of my life.

DORVAL: You're a good man Geronte.

The Game of Chess

(Picard enters)

GERONTE: My cane and hat.

DORVAL: I shall go home and wait for you there.

(Picard re-enters with the cane and hat, gives them to M Geronte and leaves again)

GERONTE: No, you wait here. I shan't be long and then we'll have dinner together.

DORVAL: I must write a letter. I need to contact my business manager. He's not in Paris at the moment.

GERONTE: You can use my room. Write your letter and give it to Picard. He'll deliver it himself. He's a good chap. Very loyal. I grumble at him sometimes but I'm really very fond of him.

DORVAL: If that's what you want, I'll wait for you here.

The Game of Chess

GERONTE: That's that, then.

DORVAL: All agreed. *(They shake hands)*

GERONTE: *(Chuckling)* My dear nephew… *(He leaves. Dalancour, hearing the last few words, is overjoyed)*

DORVAL: *(Alone)* I must be dreaming! Me, to be married. Who'd have thought it?

DALANCOUR: *(Coming forward)* I don't know how to thank you.

DORVAL: I beg your pardon?

DALANCOUR: I heard what my uncle said. He loves me after all. He's gone to see his lawyer and sort everything out. I can't tell you how relieved I am.

DORVAL: Not so fast, my friend. I'm afraid you've got the wrong end of the stick.

DALANCOUR: What do you mean?

DORVAL: I hope I'll eventually be able to sort things out with your uncle, but at the moment…

The Game of Chess

DALANCOUR: But I just heard him with my own ears. He called me his dear nephew.

DORVAL: Ah, that's not what he meant. To tell you the truth, he has done me the honour of giving me your sister's hand in marriage.

DALANCOUR: He's what? My sister's hand? What did you say?

DORVAL: Would you be happy with that?

DALANCOUR: Delighted. Delighted, my friend. You realize, of course, that as far as the dowry's concerned…

DORVAL: We don't need to talk about that.

DALANCOUR: Well then. My dear brother! Congratulations. Give me a hug.

(Enter Madame Dalancour)

Ah, my dear…

MADAME DALANCOUR: I've been waiting for you. I didn't know you'd returned.

The Game of Chess

DALANCOUR: Let me present to you, Monsieur Dorval. My brother. Angelique's fiancé.

MADAME DALANCOUR: *(Joyful)* Is this true?

DORVAL: If you approve, then it is, and my happiness is complete, madame.

MADAME DALANCOUR: Monsieur, I'm delighted. I congratulate you with all my heart. *(Aside)* It can't be true about my husband's problems, then.

DALANCOUR: *(To Dorval)* Does my sister know?

DORVAL: I don't think so.

MADAME DALANCOUR: *(Aside)* What's this? Is my husband not behind it?

DALANCOUR: Shall I fetch Angelique?

DORVAL: Not yet, monsieur. She hasn't been spoken to yet and it's important that she's happy with the arrangement.

The Game of Chess

DALANCOUR: Don't worry about that. I know my sister. You're perfect for her. Leave it to me; I'll speak to her.

DORVAL: Why don't you leave it to Monsieur Geronte?

DALANCOUR: Suit yourself.

MADAME DALANCOUR: *(Aside)* I don't understand any of this.

DORVAL: Now, I have a letter to write. Your uncle has said I can use his room and I told him I'd wait for him there. If you'll excuse me, I'll see you later.
(He goes into M Geronte's room)

MADAME DALANCOUR: Am I right in thinking that it's not you who has made this arrangement?

DALANCOUR: *(Embarrassed)* No. It's all my uncle's doing.

MADAME DALANCOUR: I see. Your uncle. Did he speak to you about it? Did he get your permission?

The Game of Chess

DALANCOUR: My permission? Didn't you just hear Dorval? Didn't you hear him asking me for my consent?

MADAME DALANCOUR: He was just being polite. Did your uncle not speak to you about this?

DALANCOUR: He hasn't yet. And that's because…

MADAME DALANCOUR: It's because he doesn't understand us at all.

DALANCOUR: It's you that doesn't understand. This is too much. I can't bear it. You're being completely unreasonable.

MADAME DALANCOUR: Me? Unreasonable? How can you say that? Oh, my darling, that's the first time you've ever said anything like that to me. You must be very upset to be so cruel.

DALANCOUR: *(Aside)* She doesn't know how right she is. *(To his wife)* My angel, I'm so sorry. I don't mean it. But you know what my uncle's like. Do you want us

The Game of Chess

                        to fall out with him? It's a good match for my sister. There's nothing we can do about it. My uncle's decided and it's a good decision. This is the best thing for everyone.

MADAME DALANCOUR: I'm glad that you're happy about it. I do respect your opinion but let me just say this. Who should make the choice of husband for your sister and arrange the wedding? Is it your uncle? Is that the proper way of doing things?

DALANCOUR: You're right. But we can't talk about it now.

MADAME DALANCOUR: One more thing. I love Angelique, you know that, but she's ungrateful. She doesn't deserve the care we take of her. Now, I know she's your sister…

DALANCOUR: What? My sister ungrateful? Why do you say such a thing?

The Game of Chess

MADAME DALANCOUR: Let's not discuss it now. I'll have a word with her and…

DALANCOUR: No. I want to know what you mean.

MADAME DALANCOUR: Leave it, my dear.

DALANCOUR: I want to know.

MADAME DALANCOUR: Well, if you insist. Your sister…

DALANCOUR: Well? Go on.

MADAME DALANCOUR: Your sister takes your uncle's side against us.

DALANCOUR: In what way?

MADAME DALANCOUR: She told me that your business affairs are in trouble and that…

DALANCOUR: My business affairs? What does she know about my business affairs? And you believed her?

The Game of Chess

MADAME DALANCOUR: No, I didn't. But she seems to believe it and she said it in such as way as to indicate that she thinks it's all my fault. Or least that I'm partly responsible.

DALANCOUR: You? She thinks that?

MADAME DALANCOUR: Don't get upset, my dear. She's young…

DALANCOUR: *(Agitated)* Oh, my darling wife.

MADAME DALANCOUR: Don't let it upset you. She's just a girl. It doesn't bother me. What does disturb me is that your uncle is behind all this.

DALANCOUR: Oh no, my uncle's not bad. He just…

MADAME DALANCOUR: Not bad? He's an interfering, insufferable old so and so. But, for your sake, I'll overlook it.

SERVANT: *(Entering)* A letter for you, monsieur. *(Dalancour takes it)*

The Game of Chess

MADAME DALANCOUR: Who is it from?

DALANCOUR: *(Aside, agitated)* Let me see. From my lawyer. *(he retires and reads the letter)*

MADAME DALANCOUR: *(Aside)* He looks upset. Who can it be from?

DALANCOUR: *(Turning white)* It's all over.

MADAME DALANCOUR: *(Aside)* I'm frightened. What can have happened?

DALANCOUR: *(Aside)* What will become of us? My poor wife. I can't tell her the truth.

MADAME DALANCOUR: My dearest, tell me what it is. You look so troubled. Whatever can be the matter?

DALANCOUR: Here, read. It's time you knew the truth. *(He hands her the letter and leaves hurriedly)*

MADAME DALANCOUR: I fear the worst. *(She reads)* "All is lost, monsieur. Your creditors won't

The Game of Chess

give way..." Oh, so it's all true. *(She reads in silence)* My husband in debt... in danger of going to prison! How can this be? He's never been extravagant. He doesn't waste his money gambling or mixing with the wrong people... Could it be my fault, after all? Goodness, it's all coming clear. Angelique's attitude, Monsieur Geronte's hatred. The contempt he's always shown for me. It's like a veil lifting. It's both my husband's fault and my own. He loves me so much and has never denied me anything. And I had no idea of the consequences. What are we to do? *(She thinks)* His uncle. It's the only solution. I must go to him, throw myself at his feet and beg forgiveness. But will that have any effect? He's so fierce, so inflexible. I don't know if I have the strength. What does it matter? These are desperate times. What's a little humiliation, when my husband's in such danger? Yes, it's the right thing to do. I must go to Monsieur Geronte and ask his pardon. *(She goes to M Geronte's room)*

The Game of Chess

MARTON: *(Entering)* What are you doing here, madame? Your husband's in a state of despair.

MADAME DALANCOUR: Heavens! I must go to him. *(Leaves)*

MARTON: *(Alone)* What a mess! It's chaos. Well, she's having to face the consequences of her actions now. What have I said all along? *(Enter Valere)* Who's this? Ah, monsieur, what are you doing here? It's not a good time. The house is in uproar.

VALERE: I'm sure it is. I've just come from Dalancour's lawyer, so I know what's going on. I've come to offer my support to Angelique's brother.

MARTON: That's very good of you, monsieur. Such generosity deserves to be rewarded.

VALERE: Is Monsieur Geronte at home?

MARTON: No, I believe he's out seeing *his* lawyer.

The Game of Chess

VALERE: His lawyer?

MARTON: Yes, he has business affairs too, you know. What do you want with the master?

VALERE: I'm concerned about Monsieur Dalancour. Here I am, single, wealthy and in love with Angelique. I am going to offer to marry her without a dowry. I have plenty for both of us.

MARTON: That's very generous of you, monsieur.

VALERE: Do you think he'll accept?

MARTON: I don't see why not. He said he wants to marry her off.

VALERE: But won't he want to choose her husband himself?

MARTON: *(After a moment's thought)* That could be.

The Game of Chess

VALERE: Do I have a hope?

MARTON: I can't see why not. One moment, monsieur. *(Calling)* Angelique, here if you please.

ANGELIQUE: *(Entering)* I'm so frightened…

VALERE: What is it, my love?

ANGELIQUE: My poor brother.

MARTON: How is he doing?

ANGELIQUE: He's a little calmer.

MARTON: Listen, mademoiselle. Monsieur Valere has a plan. Oh, he's such a good young man.

VALERE: *(Low, to Marton)* Please don't say anything just yet.

MARTON: But first he has to speak to your uncle.

ANGELIQUE: That's easier said than done.

The Game of Chess

MARTON: Ssh, there's someone coming. *(Dorval comes from M Geronte's room)* It's Monsieur Dorval. *(To Valere)* Let's go to my room. We can talk there.

VALERE: *(To Angelique)* If you see your brother…

MARTON: *(Pulling them apart)* Come, monsieur. *(Marton and Valere leave)*

ANGELIQUE: *(Alone)* I must go back to my brother.

DORVAL: Ah! Mademoiselle.

ANGELIQUE: Monsieur.

DORVAL: Have you seen your uncle? Has he said anything to you?

ANGELIQUE: I saw him this morning.

DORVAL: Before he went out?

ANGELIQUE: Yes, monsieur.

DORVAL: And has he returned?

The Game of Chess

ANGELIQUE: I don't know.

DORVAL: *(Aside)* Good. She doesn't know anything yet.

ANGELIQUE: Excuse me, monsieur. Is there anything I should know?

DORVAL: Your uncle's very fond of you, you know.

ANGELIQUE: My uncle's a good man.

DORVAL: He's very interested in your happiness.

ANGELIQUE: I believe he is.

DORVAL: He's thinking of finding you a husband. *(Silence)* Did you know that? *(Silence)* How do you feel about that?

ANGELIQUE: If it pleases my uncle...

DORVAL: Shall I let you in to a secret?

The Game of Chess

ANGELIQUE: *(Curious)* If you wish to, monsieur.

DORVAL: Your uncle has already decided on a husband for you.

ANGELIQUE: *(Aside)* Oh heavens! Who can it be?

DORVAL: *(Aside)* She's overjoyed.

ANGELIQUE: *(Trembling)* Dare I ask….?

DORVAL: Ask what, mademoiselle?

ANGELIQUE: … the young man's name?

DORVAL: The young man's name?

ANGELIQUE: Yes. Do you know him?

DORVAL: But… what if it were not a *young* man?

ANGELIQUE: *(Aside)* Heavens!

DORVAL: You're a sensible girl… and you trust your uncle, don't you?

The Game of Chess

ANGELIQUE: You don't think my uncle means to sacrifice me, do you?

DORVAL: Sacrifice you?

ANGELIQUE: I haven't been asked. How could he have got this idea about some old man? My uncle is good. It must have been someone else who's put this idea into his mind.

DORVAL: Old man? I didn't say he was old. What would you say if it were my idea?

ANGELIQUE: Yours, Monsieur Dorval? Thank heavens for that!

DORVAL: Why thanks heavens?

ANGELIQUE: You are so kind and reasonable. If it were your idea, this old man, then I know you'd be able to change my uncle's mind.

DORVAL: But… mademoiselle…

ANGELIQUE: Yes, Monsieur Dorval?

The Game of Chess

DORVAL: *(Kindly)* Is there someone else you have in mind?

ANGELIQUE: *(Shyly)* Oh, monsieur…

DORVAL: I understand.

ANGELIQUE: Please help me, monsieur.

DORVAL: *(Aside)* I can see how it is. *(Sadly)* She can't love me. It was foolish of me to think she could. It hasn't even entered her mind that it's me. Ah well, so be it.

ANGELIQUE: Monsieur Dorval, you don't say anything.

DORVAL: Mademoiselle Angelique…

ANGELIQUE: Do you have some personal interest in all this?

DORVAL: Perhaps a little.

ANGELIQUE: I warn you, I will hate him, whoever he is.

The Game of Chess

DORVAL: *(Aside)* The poor girl! I can't go through with this.

ANGELIQUE: Please, monsieur, help me.

DORVAL: Of course I will… I promise… I'll talk to your uncle. I'll do all I can to make sure you don't have to marry someone you don't want to.

ANGELIQUE: *(Joyfully)* Oh, Monsieur Dorval, I do love you!

DORVAL: *(Resigned)* Dear child.

ANGELIQUE: You are so good and kind. I think of you as a father. *(She takes his hand)*

DORVAL: My darling girl.

GERONTE: *(Entering)* My children! I'm so delighted to see this. Bravo! *(Angelique retires horrified. Dorval smiles)* What's all this? Not embarrassed are you? No need to be shy in front of me. *(To Dorval)* Well done, old man. *(To Angelique)* Come, embrace your fiancé.

The Game of Chess

ANGELIQUE: *(Horrified)* I think I understand!

DORVAL: *(Aside)* I think I've been found out.

GERONTE: *(To Angelique)* No need for all this modesty. Just because I'm here, you don't need to pretend. *(Impatiently)* Come here, both of you. Come on!

DORVAL: *(Laughing)* Hasty as usual, my friend.

GERONTE: That's right. Laugh. Show your happiness. That's what I want to see. But don't make me angry. Come here, both of you. There's something I want to say.

DORVAL: Perhaps you should listen first.

GERONTE: Come here girl. *(Tries to take Angelique by the hand)*

ANGELIQUE: *(Crying)* No, please, uncle.

GERONTE: What's the matter with you? Why the tears? *(Takes her hand and leads her forward)* Here, my friend, I give you my niece.

The Game of Chess

DORVAL: If I may speak…

GERONTE: Silence!

ANGELIQUE: Dear Uncle…

GERONTE: You too! *(Quietly)* I've been to my lawyer and everything's arranged. He's bringing the contract here and we'll all sign it.

DORVAL: Please, my friend, just listen will you..

GERONTE: As for the dowry, my brother was foolish enough to leave it in his son's hands. Never mind that, we'll…

DORVAL: Will you stop , please!

GERONTE: What? What is it?

DORVAL: There's something that… Angelique has to say to you.

ANGELIQUE: *(Terrified)* Me, monsieur?

GERONTE: I don't know what she has to say. I've made all the arrangements. It's

The Game of Chess

	all settled. And it's all been done for her good.
DORVAL:	I have something to say, as well.
GERONTE:	And what do you have to say?
DORVAL:	This marriage can't take place.
GERONTE:	WHAT? *(Both Angelique and Dorval leap back in fear)* But you gave your word of honour.
DORVAL:	Yes, but if you remember, I gave a condition.
GERONTE:	*(Turning on Angelique)* Is this your doing? You ungrateful girl. If I thought…
DORVAL:	No, Geronte, you're wrong.
GERONTE:	So, it's you who is abusing my friendship, is it? *(Angelique takes the opportunity to escape)*
DORVAL:	Please, will you let someone else speak?

The Game of Chess

GERONTE: I don't want any excuses. I'm a man of honour and if you were too… *(he turns and sees Angelique has gone)* Angelique!

DORVAL: What an impossible man. He always goes too far. *(Leaves hurriedly)*

GERONTE: Where is she? *(Noticing Dorval's gone)* What the…? Dorval! Dorval, my friend. Now, where's he got to? Hello! Anyone there? Picard! Marton! Where the devil is everyone? Picard! Anyone!

PICARD: *(Entering)* Monsieur.

GERONTE: You rogue. Where have you been?

PICARD: I'm sorry. Here I am.

GERONTE: You wretch. How many times have I called you?

PICARD: I'm sorry.

GERONTE: Ten times, at least.

The Game of Chess

PICARD: *(Aside)* He's in a right old mood.

GERONTE: Have you seen Dorval?

PICARD: Yes, monsieur.

GERONTE: Where is he?

PICARD: He's gone, monsieur.

GERONTE: Gone? What do you mean gone?

PICARD: Gone, as in he was here and now he's not.

GERONTE: Are you trying to be funny? *(Advances on Picard threateningly, making him back off)* Is this how you talk to your master?

PICARD: Are you dismissing me, monsieur?

GERONTE: What are you talking about, you rogue? *(Lunges for him, causing him to fall backwards over the chair. M Geronte immediately runs to his aid)* Are you alright?

The Game of Chess

PICARD: *(In pain)* You've hurt me, monsieur. I think I'm crippled.

GERONTE: *(Earnestly)* What can I say? Can you walk?

PICARD: *(Limping)* I think so.

GERONTE: *(Brusquely)* Off with you then.

PICARD: *(Sadly) Are* you dismissing me, monsieur?

GERONTE: What? No, of course not. Go home to your wife. Get her to look at that leg and, here, you'll need this for the doctor. *(Hands him his purse)*

PICARD: *(Aside, moved)* What a master!

GERONTE: Here take it.

PICARD: That won't be necessary, monsieur.

GERONTE: Take it!

PICARD: But, monsieur…

The Game of Chess

GERONTE: *(Sharply)* Are you refusing my money? Is this pride? Are you angry with me? I didn't do it deliberately. Please forgive me. And take the money. You'll offend me, otherwise.

PICARD: *(Taking the money)* Just for you, then, monsieur. You're very kind.

GERONTE: Get off with you, then.

PICARD: Yes, monsieur. *(Limps off)*

GERONTE: Take care, now. Here, use my cane.

PICARD: But...

GERONTE: Take it, I tell you.

PICARD: *(Taking the cane)* What kindness! *(Leaves)*

GERONTE: *(Alone)* That's the first time I've ever... damn my temper! *(Paces)* It's all Dorval's fault.

The Game of Chess

MARTON: *(Entering)* Are you ready for dinner, monsieur?

GERONTE: Leave me alone! *(Goes hurriedly to his room and locks the door after him)*

MARTON: *(Alone)* Fine! That's the way things are. There's nothing I can do for Angelique at the moment. I'd better tell Monsieur Valere that it's best if he leaves.

End of Act Two

The Game of Chess

Act Three

(Marton and Picard enter from separate doors)

MARTON: You're back, then.

PICARD: Yes, limping a bit but it's nothing. It was the shock more than anything. But the master didn't need to give me the money. Poor thing, I've never seen such repentance.

MARTON: He's a good man. Why does he have to lose his temper like that?

PICARD: We all do it sometimes but not everyone's got his kind nature.

MARTON: Go and see him. He still hasn't eaten, you know.

PICARD: Why not?

The Game of Chess

MARTON: Oh, you have no idea what's been going on in this house.

PICARD: I know enough. I met your nephew just now, so I came back. Does the master know what's happened?

MARTON: I don't think so.

PICARD: He won't take it well.

MARTON: I know. I'm afraid for poor Angelique.

PICARD: And what of Monsieur Valere?

MARTON: He's still here and he won't leave. He's comforting Monsieur and Madame Dalancour. She's crying, he's in despair and Mademoiselle Angelique does nothing but sigh. It's dreadful. They've sent me to fetch the master. I'll try speaking to him but he's still in such a temper.

PICARD: I'll go and see him. I've got to give him back his cane anyway.

The Game of Chess

MARTON: If he's calmed down a bit, you might mention the situation with his nephew.

PICARD: I will and I'll let you know what happens. Wish me luck!

MARTON: Yes, my friend, mind how you go. *(Picard quietly opens the door and goes into M Geronte's room. He gently shuts it behind him)* He's a good man, Picard. Gentle, honest and loyal. I don't know how I'd survive in this house without him.

DORVAL: *(Entering)* Marton?

MARTON: Monsieur Dorval, your servant.

DORVAL: Is Monsieur Geronte still in a temper.

MARTON: Well, you know him. If anyone does.

DORVAL: Is he still angry with me?

MARTON: With you, monsieur? Was he angry with you?

The Game of Chess

DORVAL: *(Laughing)* I'm afraid so but it'll blow over. I'm sure by now he's forgotten all about it.

MARTON: He loves and respects you, monsieur. You are almost his only friend. It's funny that... He's so intense and you're so easy-going. You go well together.

DORVAL: I think that's why we've stayed friends for so long.

MARTON: Why don't you go in and see him?

DORVAL: Not yet. I have to speak to Mademoiselle Angelique first. Do you know where she is?

MARTON: She's with her brother. You know what's been going on?

DORVAL: I have a pretty good idea. Everyone's talking about it.

MARTON: And what are they saying?

The Game of Chess

DORVAL: The usual sort of thing. Friends are sympathising, enemies are gloating and the rest just turn their backs.

MARTON: I pity his poor sister.

DORVAL: Yes, I have to speak to her.

MARTON: May I ask what about? She tells me everything, you know.

DORVAL: I have just found out that a certain Monsieur Valere…

MARTON: *(Laughing)* Monsieur Valere..?

DORVAL: You know him?

MARTON: Certainly. I know all about it.

DORVAL: Good. You can help me, then.

MARTON: In any way I can, monsieur.

DORVAL: I have to reassure Angelique…

The Game of Chess

MARTON: And Valere…

DORVAL: Yes, the two of them.

MARTON: *(Smiling)* Why don't you go to Monsieur Dalancour's quarters. You'll find them both there.

DORVAL: Valere too?

MARTON: Yes, both of them.

DORVAL: Good. I'll go straight there.

MARTON: A moment. Shall I announce you?

DORVAL: *(Laughing)* I don't need to be announced to… my brother-in-law!

MARTON: Your brother-in-law?

DORVAL: Yes.

MARTON: Who do you mean?

DORVAL: Haven't you heard?

The Game of Chess

MARTON: Nothing, monsieur.

DORVAL: Well, you'll find out soon enough. *(He leaves)*

MARTON: What's he talking about?

GERONTE: *(Entering)* Stay there. I'll get someone to take the letter. No, stay, please. *(Turning and leaving the door open)* Marton!

MARTON: Here, monsieur.

GERONTE: Send a servant to me. I want a letter taken to Monsieur Dorval's house. *(Turning back towards his room)* I said stay! Good God, the man's injured and he wants to go out. *(To Marton)* Run along.

MARTON: But, monsieur…

GERONTE: Get a move on.

MARTON: But, Dorval…

The Game of Chess

GERONTE: Yes, Dorval.

MARTON: He's here.

GERONTE: Who?

MARTON: Monsieur Dorval.

GERONTE: Monsieur Dorval?

MARTON: Yes

GERONTE: Where?

MARTON: Here.

GERONTE: Dorval's here?

MARTON: Yes.

GERONTE: Where?

MARTON: In Monsieur Dalancour's room.

GERONTE: With Dalancour? Dorval with Dalancour? I see! So, that's what he's up to. Go and fetch him. Tell

The Game of Chess

	him… no, don't… send one of his servants… No! I don't want any of his people here. You go, tell him I want him here. Now. Well?
MARTON:	Do you want me to go or don't you?
GERONTE:	Go! Don't you go upsetting me. *(Marton leaves)* So, that's the way it is. Dorval's in there with my foolish nephew. He went running to him before telling me about it. I have to hear it from Picard. So, Dorval's getting cold feet. He doesn't want to be associated with a ruined man, so he goes straight to the fool himself. Why not come to me? I could have put his mind at rest. He's got nothing to fear. Is it because of my temper? He only had to wait. Surely he knows that. And, as for that nephew of mine! I hear he's now squandered everything he had. Well, that's it, as far as I'm concerned. I'll cut him off completely. *(Shouting towards Dalancour's quarters)* Yes, you can look after yourself from now on! Traitor!

The Game of Chess

Imbecile! *(Calming a little)* But what will become of him? Who cares? No concern of mine. But his sister, she worries me. She'll need looking after. She deserves a little care. My friend Dorval will marry her and see she's alright. He doesn't need to worry about the dowry. I'll look after that. The guilty can look after themselves but I'll see to the innocent.

DALANCOUR: *(Entering and throwing himself at M Geronte's feet)* Oh, uncle, please, listen to me.

GERONTE: *(Taken aback)* What's this? Get up man.

DALANCOUR: Dear uncle, I am the most wretched of men. Have pity on me, I beg you.

GERONTE: *(A little moved)* Get up, I say.

DALANCOUR: *(On his knees)* Please don't abandon me, uncle. You are so good and kind. My only fault has been weakness. All I have done wrong is love my wife

The Game of Chess

too much. I know I should have come to you in the first place. I thought I could sort out my problems myself but they've got the better of me. And now I need your help. Dear uncle, I beg you, for the sake of the family, look on me kindly.

GERONTE: *(Slowly being won round)* What? You dare to come to me now…

DALANCOUR: It's not the loss of the money. It's more important than that. It's the loss of my honour. I don't want anything for us. I just want to protect the family honour. If you help me out, I promise my wife and I will learn our lesson. From now on, we'll rely only on our love for each other and the respect due to you.

GERONTE: *(Moved)* Poor man! Come here… but, no, I'm a fool. Family honour! Stand up, you traitor. What will happen? I pay your debts and then you start all over again.

The Game of Chess

DALANCOUR: No, uncle, I promise. You'll see. My future conduct will be above reproach.

GERONTE: Future conduct! You're a miserable wretch. An infatuated fool, led a merry dance by that vain, presumptuous woman…

DALANCOUR: *(Worked up)* No, monsieur. You mustn't blame my wife. You don't know her…

GERONTE: You dare to defend her? And lie to my face? You won't get anything from me that way. Your wife? Don't mention her name in my presence. No, nothing from me. I don't want to see or hear anything of you or your wife.

DALANCOUR: Oh, uncle. You don't know how your words hurt me.

MADAME DALANCOUR: *(Entering suddenly and speaking with quiet sincerity)* Monsieur, if you believe me to be the cause of all my husband's

The Game of Chess

troubles, then only I should suffer for them. I have been ignorant of the situation up to now but that means nothing to you, it seems. I married my husband young and I've been guilty of inexperience. I've been seduced by fashion and, I have to confess, vanity. I thought I was happy and that's my greatest crime. Now, I ask you to take back your nephew. I will tear myself from him and leave this house, and so remove the cause of my husband's disgrace. One thing I ask of you, monsieur. Moderate your hatred of me. Make allowance for my age and weakness. All I have done is love my husband too much and now I ask you to take pity on him…

GERONTE: Enough madame! If you think you can win me over…

MADAME DALANCOUR: Heavens! There's no moving him. Dear Dalancour, we're lost… *(She faints into an armchair. Dalancour runs to her)*

The Game of Chess

GERONTE: Help! Someone! Marton!

MARTON: Here I am.

GERONTE: Quickly... here... help her.

MARTON: Madame, what is it?

GERONTE: *(Giving a flask to Marton)* Here, take this. Eau de cologne. How is she?

DALANCOUR: *(In tears)* Oh, uncle.

MARTON: How are you?

MADAME DALANCOUR: *(Coming round)* Monsieur, don't trouble yourself. It's only my weakness. I will recover and then leave this house.

DALANCOUR: *(Distraught)* Oh, uncle, how can you stand by...

GERONTE: Silence! *(Brusquely to Mme Dalancour)* Stay with your husband.

MADAME DALANCOUR: Oh, monsieur.

The Game of Chess

DALANCOUR: Uncle!

GERONTE: *(Serious but calm, taking them both by the hand)* Listen to me, both of you. I don't need my savings for my old age, not all of it. It will be yours one day, anyway. Have it now. But heed my words. If you waste it today, there'll be nothing for tomorrow. Learn your lesson and behave more sensibly from now on.

MADAME DALANCOUR: You are good, monsieur…

DALANCOUR: Such generosity!

GERONTE: *(Embarrassed)* That's enough!

MARTON: Monsieur Geronte…

GERONTE: You too, you old gossip.

MARTON: You've done a fine thing, master. There's one more thing. Mademoiselle Angelique…

The Game of Chess

GERONTE: Ah yes, where is she?

MARTON: She's near, master.

GERONTE: And her fiancé?

MARTON: *(Taken aback)* Her fiancé?

GERONTE: Yes, her fiancé. Is he still angry with me? Will he see me? He hasn't gone, I hope.

MARTON: *(Puzzled)* No, monsieur. He's here too.

GERONTE: Bring them to me.

MARTON: Angelique and her fiancé?

GERONTE: *(Bristling)* Yes, yes, Angelique and her fiancé.

MARTON: Right away, master. *(She approaches the door)* Come, my children.

(Enter Angelique, Valere and Dorval)

The Game of Chess

GERONTE: And who is this gentleman?

MARTON: Monsieur, I give you Angelique, her fiancé and the witness.

GERONTE: *(Puzzled, to Angelique)* Come here, my dear.

ANGELIQUE: *(To Mme Dalancour)* Dear sister, I must ask your pardon. I have misjudged you.

MARTON: I must say the same, madame.

GERONTE: *(To Dorval)* You come too, monsieur fiancé. Are you still angry with me?

DORVAL: Me, my friend?

GERONTE: Yes, you.

DORVAL: You're mistaken. I'm only the witness.

GERONTE: The witness?

The Game of Chess

DORVAL: Yes, let me explain. If you'd allowed me to speak before…

GERONTE: Explain? What is there to explain?

DORVAL: Listen, my friend. You know Valere. His father was our friend. He knows all about the goings-on in this house and he's come to offer his fortune to Monsieur Dalancour and his hand to Mademoiselle Angelique. It's clear they love each other and he's prepared to marry her without a dowry. You understand these things; please give them your blessing.

GERONTE: *(Angry, to Angelique)* So, there's no-one? That's what you told me, and you deceived me. No, this won't do. You're all trying to get one over on me. I won't have it.

ANGELIQUE: *(Crying)* Dear uncle.

VALERE: *(Passionate and imploring)* Please, monsieur…

The Game of Chess

DALANCOUR: You are so good…

MADAME
DALANCOUR: So generous…

MARTON: My dear master…

GERONTE: Damn this temper of mine. I can't stay angry with you. *(They surround him and entreat him)* Enough! Take her. Do what you want. And then leave me in peace. *(They all surge forward to thank him)* Go! Go! Where's Picard?

PICARD: Here, monsieur.

GERONTE: Arrange for this lot to have supper in my rooms and then get rid of them. *(To Dorval)* And you, my friend, before then, let's sit and finish that game of chess.

End of the play

ABOUT THE AUTHOR

Simon Thomas has written about opera and theatre for 10 years, contributing reviews and features to publications and online magazines. He has studied the life and works of Goldoni for over 30 years and is the author of The Theatre of Carlo Goldoni. He also has a keen interest in the plays of Samuel Beckett and Henrik Ibsen. He was Opera Editor of Whatsonstage.com, the UK's leading theatre website, from 2009 to 2011.

You can follow him on Twitter @sthomasreviews

Made in the USA
Monee, IL
20 May 2022